GREAT ARTISTS

LEONARDO DA VINCI

Maria Teresa Zanobini Leoni

ENCHANTED LION BOOKS
New York

Leonardo da Vinci

IN THESE YEARS

1452 Born on 15 April at Anchiano near Vinci (outside Florence), Leonardo is the illegitimate son of Ser Pietro di Antonio, a notary. He is raised in his father's home.

1469 Following the death of Leonardo's grandfather Antonio, the family moves to Florence. Young Leonardo is apprenticed to Verrocchio, whose workshop excels in sculpture, goldsmithery, and painting, as well as studies in geometry, physics, and the natural sciences. Other apprentices include the Pollaiolo brothers, Botticelli, Perugino, and Lorenzo di Credi. Lorenzo the Magnificent will become the ruler of Florence.

The Supremacy of Painting

In the 16th-century debate over which art was supreme, Leonardo supports painting as an objective depiction of reality. His writings reflect an array of interests, but painting is clearly his first love.

From his earliest youth, Leonardo da Vinci (Anchiano 1452-Amboise, France, 1519) was fascinated by the challenges of depicting nature, which ranged from the study of the gradations of light and shadow, to the effects created by multiple light sources upon figures, or reflected light upon faces and objects.

He devoted special study to the portrayal of landscapes, and was interested in the optics and special effects of things seen from a distance.

He therefore tried to outstrip even the most advanced teachings of the finest workshops of Florence, where he had gained his foundations in anatomy, human proportion, perspective, and artistic techniques. Many of his works, in fact, bear the marks of his tireless study and repeated revisions; as a result they often seem unfinished, at least in conventional terms. His relentless need to retouch paintings in a quest for perfection meant that he might even change technique from one revision to the next.

Although few of his works survive, the immense complexity of those that do makes each a world unto itself, blending scientific observation and careful experimentation, recorded in notes and sketches of varying degrees of precision. Each painting should be seen as an ultimate summary of his work and his experience as a draftsman, an observer, a painter, and a profound artist.

The features of this supposed *Self Portrait* by Leonardo closely resemble the wood-block engraving on the frontispiece of "Life of Leonardo" in the second edition (1568) of Giorgio Vasari's great literary and historical work, *The Lives of the Artists*. The same features appear on a character in the entourage of Pope Leo X, depicted by Vasari himself in a fresco in the Palazzo Vecchio.

These features recur as well in two frescoes by Raphael in the Vatican *Stanze* (or rooms), in likenesses of Plato and David.

Michelangelo, too, evoked Leonardo in a drawing. Since there is no evidence to the contrary, let us accept this magnificent drawing as an authentic self-portrait. Here, Leonardo portrays himself with a discerning, far-seeing gaze, and the eyes of a deep thinker. His face bears the clear marks of old age, taken not simply as a process of physical decay but also as the attainment of the fullness of wisdom.

Self-Portrait
Red crayon on paper
13 x 8¹/₂ in.
(33.3 x 21.4 cm.),
Biblioteca Nazionale,
Turin.

This drawing offers the earliest certain documentation of Leonardo's work as an artist. The writing is, as usual, reversed, but looks more like a merchant's bookkeeping, than the flowing script of a humanist scholar. The setting, while not specified, is certainly the Arno Valley.

Landscape in the Arno Valley

Having just turned twenty, and newly and formally accredited as a painter, Leonardo continued to work for Verrocchio, as is shown by his contribution to the *Baptism of Christ* (1473–1476; see pp. 8–9). The landscape depicted in that work (just above the heads of the two angels) must have been eagerly discussed by the painters in the workshop, including Botticelli. In this drawing from 1473, Leonardo works to depict a river landscape with rocky hillsides in the foreground and broad fields in the distance. The eye runs upward from the hill at lower right, to the semicircular arrangement of rocks, covered with trees and bushes; it then drops–with the plunging waterfall–to the curve of the river, which then flows on, running past the rocky mount topped by a castle. Here the eye takes a new direction into the distance, following the lines dividing the fields, some running sharply to the left,

others toward the center. In the distance, on the right, the horizon is marked by faintly drawn hills.

Annunciation

In the dawn light, in the garden of a wealthy Tuscan villa from the early Quattrocento, an angel appears to Mary to announce that She will soon become a mother. The young woman sits in a chair that is covered by the folds of Her ample, ultramarine mantle, beneath which we see a red dress, fastened above the waist with a girdle. The figure of the Virgin stands out against dark walls, and is framed by light ashlar quoins. Beyond the low garden wall, pines, cypresses, and other trees are silhouetted against the pale-blue sky. The Madonna rests Her hand on a book on a lectern, whose design is a tribute to Verrocchio. In the distance lies a port city with ships and boats,

and, in the far background, we see craggy peaks. The composition features a straightforward perspective, with a vanishing point to the left of the little mountain, guiding the eye into the distance. The perspective is simple and unified, yet vivid details continually distract: the rich folds of draped cloth, the flowered lawn, the interlocking gazes, the eloquent gestures of the hands, the beautiful lily held between the angel's fingers, and the various shapes of the trees. Every feature of the composition is bathed in the crystalline dawn light that streams from the left, joining and linking all these details in a manifold and mystical harmony.

Annunciation
1472–75, oil and tempera on panel, 41 x 85$^{1}/_{2}$ in. (104 x 217 cm.) *Uffizi Gallery, Florence.*

1472 Leonardo is listed as "maestro" in the Company of Painters, the artist's guild.

—He marks this year on the pen-and-ink *Drawing of a Landscape*, now in the Uffizi.

1475 He paints the portrait of Ginevra de' Benci, now in the National Gallery, Washington.

1476 Lorenzo the Magnificent admits Leonardo to the Garden of San Marco, where he comes into contact with the Medici cultural milieu, developing his scientific interests, both experimental and theoretical, as well as his love of mathematics.

1477 In January he is commissioned to paint an altarpiece for the Chapel of St. Bernard (now lost), in Palazzo Vecchio, a sign of his growing fame as a painter. As an engineer, he proposes raising the Baptistery of San Giovanni in Florence, in order to add a basement with stairs.

The Baptism of Christ

This painting, generally attributed to Leonardo, was clearly the work of several artists. It may have been a practice piece for a number of pupils in Verrocchio's workshop, where it remained for several years after 1470. X-rays and reflectance tests done during a recent restoration confirm that this was the case. Three distinct techniques have been identified, and Leonardo is thought to have painted: the final, oil version of Christ, using his fingertips to give nuance to the flesh tones; the landscape, with its staggered planes of perspective; the water in which John the Baptist's foot is submerged; the rocks and trees above the heads of the two angels (the angel on the left was certainly by his hand). These elements clearly bear the mark of Leonardo's style, with its staccato vibrancy, its fluent spaciousness, and the vigor that echoes throughout the composition. Even the landscape, originally constructed in accordance with a rigid geometric layout, becomes an open field in which the eye moves freely from foreground—where the main event takes place—out to the remote distance.

Leonardo in Verrocchio's Workshop

Art critics working in the 19th-century tradition, influenced by the "theory of the genius," tended to give Leonardo a unique status as an innovator who, alone, conceived his new style. Many features of his work, however, when examined with a colder eye, tell us that he consciously and skilfully absorbed many elements of Verrocchio's style, preserving them as part of his own distinctive manner.

The Baptism of Christ
1475–1478, oil and tempera on panel,
61³/₄ x 59¹/₄ in. (157 x 151 cm.) *Uffizi Gallery, Florence.*

SFUMATO

The style of *chiaroscuro* used by Leonardo in this painting heralds the exceedingly smooth transitions from light to shadow in his later works, a style known as *sfumato*. In painting and drawing, *sfumato* describes a transition from light to dark so smooth and gradual as to be imperceptible. The use of *sfumato* tends virtually to eliminate outlines, and is generally thought to originate with Leonardo.

Madonna of the Carnation

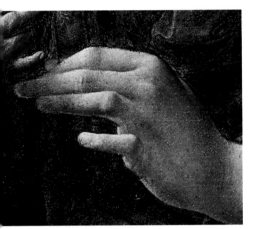

The portrayal of the two figures in an interior, using an intricate interweaving of shadows and semi-darkness, as well as multiple light sources, both direct (frontal and from above) and from behind (through the windows), was well-suited to the complex effects desired, especially the emphasis on plastic form. Baby Jesus reaches out to the Madonna; her hand, holding a carnation, is a masterful piece of design as well as an exercise in the optics and physics of lighting, shaped by an array of shadows, half-shadows, reflections, and highlights.

The same scientific treatment is devoted to the folds of cloth, a special interest of Leonardo's, and the flowers in the exquisite vase.

The neckline of the Virgin's bodice is fastened with a precious jewel. Her hair is elaborately styled, with curls and elegant braids. Through the mullioned windows, we see an idealized landscape, typical of Leonardo: rocky crags flooded in dazzling light, glittering water, and detailed trees and bushes. The jagged mountain peaks in the distance are tinged with pale-blue ambient light, finally blending into the color of the sky.

In the years that Leonardo spent in Verrocchio's workshop, 1470 to 1476, painting the Madonna and Christ Child was very much the fashion. The young painter was as influenced by it as anyone, as many drawings and countless paintings from the period reveal.

Madonna of the Carnation
1478–80,
Oil on panel,
24¹/₂ x 18¹/₂ in.
(62 x 47 cm.)
Alte Pinakothek, Munich.

IN THESE YEARS

1481 The artist is commissioned to paint the *Adoration of the Magi* (unfinished, now in the Uffizi Gallery). —Disappointed at being overlooked in the commissions for the decoration of the Sistine Chapel in Rome, Leonardo writes to Lodovico Sforza ("the Moor") in Milan, offering his services as an engineer and artist.

1482 The artist leaves Florence for Milan, and finds lodgings near the gate of Porta Ticinese with two painters, the De Predis brothers. He remains in Milan until 1499.

Madonna with a Flower (Benois Madonna)

One of Leonardo's few finished works, though clearly revised more than once, this painting represents a significant step in the stylistic transition that takes place between the Uffizi *Annunciation* and the *Adoration of the Magi* (unfinished). Here the Virgin Mary is playing with the Christ Child, showing him a four-petaled flower, a foreshadowing of the Crucifixion, in keeping with the esoteric symbolism of Marsilio Ficino, then fashionable at the Medici court. She is elegantly attired; a rock-crystal brooch, set with pearls, gleams on her chest. Her elaborately curled hair leaves her high forehead uncovered; it reflects the light. The folds of her garments are shaped by the movements of her body, so that the fabric ranges from compact wrinkles around her bent elbow to broad folds across her knee. The array of light effects that Leonardo studied carefully in his sketches of drapery move and shift across her dress. The composition focuses on the intertwined hands of Christ Child and Madonna. They are depicted in an interior; a diffuse light is further illuminated by multiple sources: from behind and above, and from the left. In the background, on the left, hangs a bronze-green curtain, possibly enclosing a four-poster bed. Evening light streams in the window on the right, backlighting the two figures. Shadows lap at the figures with varying intensity, enlivening them with vital energy. Every detail takes on a sculptural depth, unprecedented in Florentine painting; such depth would become a powerful influence.

Attribution of this painting to Leonardo is almost unanimously accepted, and is based on a note in his hand, on a drawing now in the Uffizi (no. 446). The note is fragmentary, but it does tell us that he began work on two paintings of the Virgin Mary in late 1478. The model for the Madonna may have been the third wife of Leonardo's father.

Madonna with a Flower
1478–1482,
Oil on panel,
transferred to canvas,
19 x 12^1/$_4$ in.
(48 x 31 cm.)
Hermitage, St. Petersburg

THE NATIVITY OF CHRIST ACCORDING TO LEONARDO

Before Leonardo, the theme of the Nativity was linked with the Annunciation to the Shepherds, or else with the Adoration of the Magi. Leonardo, now twenty-nine and an experienced artist, develops a new interpretation of the theme, proving his ability to narrate a complex and significant story. He chooses to portray the Epiphany, or the manifestation of Christ to humanity, marking the transition from a state of barbarism (note battle between horsemen and wild beasts at top right) to the civilizing influence of the coming of Christ.

The Adoration of the Magi

The execution of this panel painting (unfinished) went well beyond a two-dimensional portrayal. The outlines, of varying thickness, proliferate until they achieve effects of light and volume. Here and there, we find touches of color, brushstrokes of white lead, and layer upon layer of red and greenish lacquers, creating luminous highlights. On the right, a standing figure colored chiefly in shades of green and brown leads us to believe that those would have been the programmatic hues of the finished work. The Madonna and Child form the focal point of the pyramid-shaped composition; surrounding and surmounting them are some sixty figures, clustered in separate scenes. In the top right corner, against a rocky background, horsemen fight savagely, representing barbaric humanity. On the left, against an architectural background, a master-builder supervises laborers repairing the ruins of a building, symbolizing the reconstruction of a new world. Riders emerge from the arches of the building, leading a procession that wends its way down to mingle with the dramatically posed figures that cluster around the central group in the foreground. Among the many anonymous faces, we can make out Dante and Virgil (representing the Christian and pagan cultures, the present and the past). The pageant concludes at the bottom right with the well-defined figure of the young man mentioned above (a self portrait?), and a corresponding older figure, lost in thought, in the left foreground. Against the dark background, the fully lit

Adoration of the Magi
1481–1482,
oil on panel,
96³/₄ x 95³/₄ in.
(246 x 243 cm.) *Uffizi Gallery, Florence.*

figure of the Virgin Mary emerges, stylistically similar to other depictions of the Madonna by Leonardo. This work—in its complexity, its innovative narrative approach, and its extraordinary use of light—constitutes a genuine manifesto of the modern age.

In the second decade of the fifteenth century, the Florentine architect Filippo Brunelleschi laid down the mathematical and geometric laws governing perspective, making possible the lifelike and reliable depiction of spatial depth on flat surfaces. These rules envisage a single vanishing-point upon which all orthogonals converge. This is precisely what we see in Leonardo's drawings.

Perspective Study for the Adoration of the Magi

Many of Leonardo's sketches of the Madonna, of young male nudes (potential angels or shepherds), and of the faces of character types and animals are preparatory to the *Adoration of the Magi*. This sketch, now in the Uffizi, is a final perspective layout for the upper part of the painting. The figures are barely sketched in, but we already can clearly see the

cluster of riders on the right, the focal point of the lines of perspective; on the left we can see outlines of a building and its two staircases crowded with workmen climbing up and down. Leonardo's debt to the classical world, especially the Hellenistic

world, is evident in his use of classical architecture, his depiction of battling horsemen and rearing horses, as well as in the dramatic energy that powers the composition. Rather than imagining a hypothetical journey to Rome, we may attribute his classicism to his contact with Florentine humanist culture and its tendency to model itself on the classics. From this culture, the artist develops a style so distinctive that Vasari in his biography calls him "the founder of the third age," which is to say, the modern one.

Saint Jerome

The scene is set in the mouth of a cave; in the distance, on the left, we see a rocky landscape shrouded in mist, quite similar to the background in the *Mona Lisa*. A pale light filters through jumbled pieces of rock on the right, an effect achieved by leaving the gesso ground (a layer covering the wooden panel designed to support underdrawing and paint) uncovered. Through this window-like opening, we see the façade of a church. The lion, sketched in outline, lies stretched out before the saint, looking anything but tame. Its massive bulk, the sharp silhouette of its head, its open mouth and long, curving tail serve as a counterweight to the figure of the saint. The depiction of Saint Jerome, with his head twisted to the side, straining away from his torso, and with one arm outstretched and one knee thrust forward, is forceful. It is precisely a sense of dynamic movement that Leonardo strove to convey here. That is what makes this work so modern and innovative. It will be widely admired and copied by generations of artists to come. The anatomy of the saint's body is clearly in keeping with the rules of proportion that Leonardo had devised after prolonged study, alongside his work on perspective. The unfinished aspect of this painting helps us to understand Leonardo's unusual working methods, which include his technique of drawing in paint, and his approach to illuminating and modeling his figures through light so that they twist dynamically upon themselves.

The kneeling saint implores forgiveness from the Crucifix turned slightly before him. In his right hand he grasps a stone with which he beats his breast, having bared it with his left hand.

Saint Jerome
ca. 1482, tempera and oil on panel, 42$^1/_2$ x 29 in. (108.2 x 73.5 cm,) *Vatican Picture Gallery, Rome.*

SANTA MARIA DELLE GRAZIE

The complex of Santa Maria delle Grazie is begun for the Dominican Friars in

1464, to plans by the architect Guiniforte Solari. Building is continued and completed by Bramante around

1495; he sets the dome atop the central-plan church and completes the cloisters. Originally the church was intended

as a mausoleum.

The Last Supper

This magnificent fresco, twice as long as it is high (it consists of two squares, side by side), forms a perfectly symmetrical design, mirrored in the architecture depicted in the painting. The table around which the animated scene takes place seems to suggest that the fixed nature of the world is about to be thrown into turmoil by the fateful announcement of the Passion of the Savoir. The apostles are clustered, intently conversing, in four groups of three, almost as if to make it easier to count them. Leonardo devotes considerable time to studying each of the groups, even each figure, as is shown by his numerous preparatory sketches. Each group is rythmically arranged along the table, almost like notes on a bar of musical notation. The scene is illuminated by three sources of light—one from the front, one from the side, and one from

1) *Bartholomew*
2) *James the Less*
3) *Andrew*
4) *Peter*
5) *Judas*
6) *John*
7) *Jesus*
8) *Thomas*
9) *James the Great*
10) *Philip*
11) *Matthew*
12) *Thaddeus*
13) *Simon.*

behind—so that the room is pervaded by a soft light that reveals the alternating colors and allows us to examine the detailed depictions of the faces of the different characters. Unfortunately, the technique adopted by Leonardo has required restoration on many occasions over the centuries; in the late 20th century the fresco was cleaned and an attempt was made to save what little could still be rescued.

STUDY OF A MAN'S HEAD AND ARCHITECTURE
1495–1496, Red chalk and ink on paper
9³/₄ x 6³/₄ in. (25 x 17 cm.)
Royal Library, Windsor Castle.

Leonardo is busy with studies, drawings, and large cartoons used to transfer his ideas onto the wall from late 1495 until 1496. Among the many preparatory sketches only three heads can be attributed to him with certainty: one of St. Philip, one of Judas, and one of St. James the Greater. St. James, second to the right from Christ in the fresco, is the subject of this drawing. His sunken eyes and shaded cheeks, now barely visible in the fresco, may indicate a blush of confusion, or simply ashen pallor, at Christ's announcement of His impending betrayal.

Leonardo captures the moment when Christ announces that one of His disciples will betray Him. They all look at one another in sorrowful astonishment and fear; the expression of each reflecting his personality.

The Last Supper
1495–1497, tempera and oil on plaster, 181 x 346$^1/_2$ in. (460 x 880 cm.) *Refectory of Santa Maria delle Grazie, Milan.*

IN THESE YEARS

1483 The artist signs a contract with the Confraternity of the Conception to paint the *Virgin of the Rocks,* together with the De Predis brothers. —He begins to make sketches for a monument to Francesco Sforza.

Virgin of the Rocks

The marvelous compositional matrix intertwining the figures of the Virgin, the Infant St. John, the Christ Child, and the angel may perhaps cause us to overlook the scientific precision with which the entire work is organized, from the sophisticated pyramid-shaped arrangement of the figures to the minutely accurate depiction of botanical species. We should note the rendering of the geological power of the rock formations, in a visionary interplay of light and reflection, revealing Leonardo's propensity for reading from the great book of nature; he knowingly does much more than merely imitate, in the movements and gestures of the figures, and in his rendering of natural appearances and atmospheric references. The characters are linked one to another by their gestures and gazes, and by the complex interplay of direct and reflected light. Numerous preliminary studies of rocks, waterfowl, plants,and drapery precede the execution of the painting. Special care is devoted to the angel's head.

A copy of this painting is in the National Gallery, London.

Head of the Angel in the Virgin of the Rocks
1483, Silverpoint on paper, 7 x 6$^1/_4$ in. (18.1 x 15.9 cm.)
Biblioteca Reale, Turin.

Virgin of the Rocks
1483-1486, Oil on panel, 78 x 48$^1/_2$ in. (198 x 123 cm.)
Louvre, Paris.

With the arrival in Venice of Antonella da Messina in 1475, on his way back from Flanders, the oil portrait enters into common use as a genre unto itself. Antonello was one of the chief proponents in Italy of portraiture with the three-quarter view—against a dark background, or a landscape stretching off into the distance— derived from early 15th-century Flemish painting. The new style is willingly adopted a few years later by Leonardo. This technique allows him to delve yet more deeply into the interplay of light and shadow, and to capture psychological portraits. With oils, he is able to reconsider and revise in ways that are unthinkable in fresco painting.

Portrait of a Man, Antonello da Messina ca. 1475, Oil on panel *Borghese Gallery, Rome.*

Portrait of a Musician

The spare compositional idiom of this portrait recalls two other paintings: the celebrated *Lady with an Ermine* (in Cracow) and *La Belle Ferronnière* (in the Louvre). Here, in particular, certain fundamentally graphic elements manage to attain three-dimensional effects: the two broad orange-ochre bands are sufficient to indicate the singer's powerful chest; a narrow white collar models his round neck. The handsome youth is portrayed against a dark background, highlighting his fair skin and thrusting the figure toward us. A red cap, practically a geometric solid, perches atop his head, reiterating the figure's three-dimensional volume. A mane of curls bursts from under the cap, and is partly swallowed up by the dark background. The face is noteworthy for its rich array of nuance and shadow which create a slight tension in the facial muscles and the half-closed mouth, which suggests that the young man has just finished singing.

In the musician's hand we see a pen and a sheet of music, upon which we can read: Cant(um) Ang(elicum).

Portrait of a Musician
1482-1484, Oil on panel, 17 x 12¼ in. (43 x 31 cm.)
Ambrosian Gallery, Milan.

LODOVICO SFORZA Known as "The Moor" (1452-1508), he is the duke of Milan from 1494 to 1499, and dreams of making his city into the Athens of Italy. His court is one of the most brilliant and splendid in Europe. A munificent patron of the arts, he invites the most accomplished figures of the age, such as the mathematician Luca Pacioli, and such celebrated artists as Bernardino Zenate, Bernardino Butinone, Donato Bramante and Leonardo himself to Milan. The foremost Italian, Spanish, and Flemish musicians compose and perform music for the ducal choir.

Lady with an Ermine

There has been much speculation as to the identity of this lovely young girl, and countless conjectures concerning the presence of the ermine, possibly a symbol of chastity. The sitter is generally thought to be Cecilia Gallerani, a favorite of Lodovico the Moor. Here, as in other portraits by Leonardo, the figure is shown against a dark interior background, to great volumetric and perspectival effect. The young woman's gaze is directed offstage, as it were, to the right. Here too, as in other small-format portraits, we find— accentuated by lighting effects—linear motifs that create an impression of relief and volume: the circular shape of the pearl necklace and its shadow, the edge of the veil on her forehead, the ribbon. The dark edge of her neckline and the veil passing beneath her chin emphasize the oval of her beautiful, almost impersonal face, which reveals a certain wit and reserve. The ambiguity of her personality is further underlined by shadows from above and from the right. The hand in the foreground hints at the elongated form of the creature she is holding, and recalls the beautiful tapering fingers of Florentine sculpture.

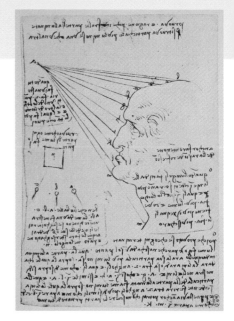

EFFECTS OF LIGHT ON A HEAD VIEWED IN PROFILE *Collection of Drawings and Prints.Uffizi, Florence.* Manuscript C (1490) contains notes *On Light and Shade,* with drawings. Leonardo studies the effects of light sources on solids, and the shadows produced. He recommends painting the walls of the studio black in order to capture the effects more successfully.

Lady with an Ermine
1488-1490, Oil on panel, 21¼ x 15¼ in., (54 x 39 cm,) *Czartoryski Museum, Cracow.*

1495 Leonardo works in Florence on the decoration of the Sala del Gran Consiglio in the Palazzo della Signoria. By the turn of the 16th century, because of the experimental technique he used to dry the painted walls, the fresco will have been lost.

—He begins work on *The Last Supper* for the refectory of Santa Maria delle Grazie in Milan; he finishes in 1497.

1496 Leonardo makes friends with the mathematician Luca Pacioli.

1498 Leonardo frescoes the Sala delle Asse in Milan's Sforza Castle.

1499 Lodovico the Moor endows a vineyard to the 'renowned painter' Leonardo, for his 'great merits'.

—King Louis XII of France marches into Italy and takes Milan. Leonardo flees the city and takes refuge in Mantua, where he makes sketches for a portrait of Isabella d'Este. He then goes to Venice.

La Belle Ferronnière
1490-1495, Oil on panel, 24½ x 17¼ in. (62 x 44 cm.) .
Louvre, Paris.

La Belle Ferronnière

A very rigorous geometric structure is used in this portrait. Leonardo adheres to his beliefs: the head is a pure geometric form, an ellipsoid, and the lady's eyes are two perfect almond-cut gems. The volume of the shoulders is clearly described by the ribbon hemming the bodice. The bun of hair gathered in the shape of an "s" just under the ear emphasizes, with its curves, the oval of the face. More than a portrait, it almost seems like a mathematical theorem. The sitter's glance avoids that of the observer, and the three-quarters view of her torso leads us to think of a sculpture in full relief, strongly illuminated, against the dark background.

1503 In Florence, Leonardo is commissioned to fresco the *Battle of Anghiari* in the Palazzo Vecchio. Michelangelo is commissioned to paint the *Battle of Cascina* there as well. For technical reasons, Leonardo's work is disastrous.

—Leonardo is appointed military engineer by Duke Valentino Borgia, to restore the fortresses of the Romagna.

1505 He returns to Milan at the invitation of the French governor, Charles d'Amboise.

1507 Francesco Melzi becomes Leonardo's pupil, and later inherits his manuscripts.

1508 Michelangelo begins work on the Sistine Chapel.

1513 Leonardo leaves Milan for Rome, in the service of Giuliano de' Medici. He produces numerous paintings, many of which have been lost.

Mona Lisa (La Gioconda)

Leonardo took his time with this panel painting. It took him more than ten years to finish it, and he saw it as solving various problems in the rendering of the transitions between light and shadow. The mysterious smile is produced by a slight parting of the lips and a faint movement of the facial muscles, depicted in the half-light. The gaze that meets the eyes of the observer is beguiling, yet the sitter retains immense dignity. In the *Anatomical Notebooks,* Leonardo rails against *"abbreviators,"* as he calls them, those who abandon themselves *"to impatience, the mother of stupidity."* This explains very well why he abandons a dark and uniform background, replacing it with one of his surreal landscapes which he had relied upon since his apprenticeship in Verrocchio's workshop.

The brushwork is very fine. The *sfumato*—obtained with layer upon layer of colorless oil-based glaze, used to create highlights and transparent depth—is especially notable in the woman's face and hands. The figure is thus given volume and rendered evanescent.

The sitter is generally identified, in accordance with Giorgio Vasari, as Monna Lisa (with one n in English), the wife of Francesco del Giocondo. In 1542 the painting is purchased by François I, King of France, for a large sum of money, and it becomes part of the collection of Fountainebleau, until it is transferred to the Louvre in 1805.

Mona Lisa (La Gioconda)
1503-1504 and 1510-1515, Oil on panel, 30¼ x 20¾ in. (77 x 53 cm.) Paris, Louvre

The landscape, wherein uncontrollable geological forces seem to have been unleashed, reflects remote cosmic upheavals which are thus explained by Leonardo: 'I find that the plains of the earth were originally covered and filled with salt waters, and the mountains—the bones of the earth— with their wide bases raised themselves and penetrated into the air, covered and clothed with much deep earth. Then the many rains, and rising of the rivers, with frequent washings despoiled in part the high peaks of the mountains; the rock was surrounded by air, and the earth of those places removed, and the earth from the plains and the high peaks of the mountains was already descended to the base, and raised the bed of the seas which surrounded them, and uncovered the plains.' We might be reading Genesis, or a page of Lucretius.

Madonna and Christ Child with St. Anne and St. John the Baptist
1500-1501, Charcoal and white lead, 62$^1/_2$ x 39$^3/_4$ in. (159 x 101 cm.), *National Gallery, London.*

St. Anne, the Madonna, and the Christ Child, with the Lamb

This painting is based on the renowned and magnificent cartoon, now in the National Gallery in London. In that cartoon, Leonardo devised a sculptural group in the classical manner, composed statically. He must have been unsatisfied with the composition for he produced further drawings and two more cartoons between the autumn of 1500 and the spring of 1501 (now lost but greatly admired by the artist's contemporaries). Leonardo works to develop a composition in which the figures form an intertwined whole, surmounted by the head of St. Anne. He finally arrives at a pyramidal arrangement of the figures, articulated in an interweaving of legs, arms, heads, and feet. Once again we glimpse the surreal landscape of the artist's youth, but here to even greater fanciful effect. The deterioration of the painting prevents us from distinguishing the numerous layers of color in the drapery. The landscape, however, remains clearly visible; it is perhaps the most complex and alluring landscape that Leonardo ever painted.

Madonna and Child with St. Anne
1510, Oil on panel, 66 x 44 in. (168 x 112 cm.)
Louvre, Paris.

IN THESE YEARS

1516 Leonardo goes to France, at the invitation of King François I, and settles

at Cloux, near Amboise, with his pupils Salai and Melzi. He devises machinery for a great ceremony honoring the king at

the castle of Argentan. **1517** He is afflicted by paralysis. **1519** Leonardo dies on 2 May, having dictated his will to his favorite

pupil Francesco Melzi. He is buried in Amboise. Later in the century, during the wars between Catholics and

Huguenots, his grave will be desecrated and his remains scattered and lost.

Saint John the Baptist

This is certainly one of the last works painted by Leonardo, at least among those that have survived. It does pose some problems in terms of attribution, especially because of the heavy yellowing of the varnish, which makes it difficult to see properly and is almost monochromatic in appearance. Further, even though there are reports of several *St. John*s in the artist's studio at Cloux, around 1517, we have no solid evidence of attribution. Nevertheless, the *sfumato* on the face, the atmosphere, and the pose of the figure are all typical of Leonardo's style. The torso of the extraordinarily youthful saint emerges from the dark background, with a twisting movement that presents a three-quarters view of the body while the head, tilted to the left

over the shoulder, presents the face frontally. Light falling from the upper left illuminates the face, shoulder, arm, and hand; the index finger points straight up to heaven. This gesture refers to a prophetic heralding of the coming of Christ. A faint cross helps to balance the somewhat uncertain gesture of the arm, which winds up on a line with the face. While the spirit and technique can certainly be ascribed to Leonardo, the execution of some portions is certainly the work of a pupil. This personage with his ambiguous smile seems less a saint than a young Florentine man of ideal beauty. This composition was very popular, and was imitated, not only by Leonardo's immediate followers, but also by Venetian painters.

FRANÇOIS I OF VALOIS (1494-1547) King of France from 1515 to his death, he saw the invasion of Italy, and especially of the Duchy of Milan, as a crucial task. He was a patron of culture and the universities. He invited many Italian artists to his court, including Leonardo, Benvenuto Cellini, and Rosso Fiorentino.

St. John the Baptist ca. 1517, Oil on panel, 27 x 22^1/$_2$ in. (69 x 57 cm.) *Louvre, Paris.*

Vitruvian Man

This drawing illustrates a passage in Vitruvius's *De Architectura*, and represents a man in two different positions, set in a square and a circle. The body inscribed in the square is as tall as the span of his outstretched arms. His navel marks the center of the circle. Placing the point of the compass on it, we see that the circumference touches the fingers and toes of the outspread limbs. For Leonardo, moreover, the height of the figure corresponds to eight times the height of the head, as we can see from this drawing. In many of his writings, Leonardo asserts that it is essential in painting for the limbs to have a specific direct proportion to the height. Experimental observation, however, later persuaded him to take movement into account when painting human figures, which he realized changed those direct proportions, along with the distance of the observer from the subject, and the effects of light. Finally, the various personal characteristics of the subject should not be overlooked. Leonardo may be regarded as the first naturalist who consciously sought the key to understanding and depicting anatomical features in mathematics. His faith in mathematics was not limited to its usefulness; he also saw it as a means by which to activate the harmonious correspondence between man—understood as a microcosm—and the cosmos as a whole.

Vitruvian Man
ca. 1490. Mixed media on paper, 13^1/$_2$ x 9^1/$_2$ in. (34.3 x 24.5 cm.) *Accademia, Venice.*

Index of Leonardo's works:

*Page numbers in bold refer to illustrations of the work in question.

First American edition published in 2003 by
Enchanted Lion Books
115 West 18th Street, New York, NY 10011
Copyright © 2002 McRae Books Srl
English language text copyright © 2003 McRae Books Srl
All rights reserved
Printed and bound in the Slovak Republic
Library of Congress Cataloging-in-Publication Data
Leoni Zanobini, Maria Teresa.
  Leonardo da Vinci / Maria Teresa Zanobini Leoni—1st American ed.
    p. cm — (Great artists)
  Includes index.
  Summary: Discusses the style and technique of the Italian artist and inventor Leonardo da Vinci.
  ISBN 1-59270-007-1
    1. Leonardo, da Vinci, 1452-1519—Criticism and interpretation—Juvenile literature. [1. Leonardo, da Vinci, 1452-1519. 2. Artists. 3 Painting, Italian.] I. Leonardo, da Vinci, 1452-1519. II. Title. III. Great artists (Enchanted Lion Books)

N6923.L33L47 2003
709'.2—dc21   2003049057
The series "Great Artists" was created and produced by
McRae Books Srl, Borgo Santa Croce, 8, Florence, Italy
Info@mcraebooks.com
Series Editor: Roberto Carvalho de Magalhães / Text: Maria Teresa Zanobini Leoni
Design: Marco Nardi · Layouts: Laura Ottina
The Publisher thanks the following archives, which authorized the reproduction of the artworks depicted in this volume: Scala Group, Florence (3, 4-5, 6-7, 10-11, 12, 15, 16-17, 19, 20-21, 23, 24, 25, 26, 27, 28, 29, 30, 31, 33, 35, 37, 39), Bridgeman Art Library, London (9, 34). and the CD-Rom *The Science of Memory* (1998), a vast collection of texts of museum studies.

Cover: **La Belle Ferronnière,** 1490-1495, *(detail)*

Page 1: Raphael, **Schools of Athens,** 1510-11, believed to be a portrait of Leonardo *(detail)*